what
kids do

ME MARY ENGELBREIT

www.maryengelbreit.com

03 04 05 06 07 LEO 10 9 8 7 6 5 4 3 2

ISBN: 0-7407-3907-7
Library of Congress PCN: 2003106543

Illustrations by Mary Engelbreit
Design by Stephanie R. Farley
Edited by Polly Blair

illustrated by
mary engelbreit

Andrews McMeel
Publishing

Kansas City

What do kids do?

They get dirty.

They wish on stars.

They giggle till they fall off their chairs.

They make their parents crazy.

They make their parents proud.

And they also grow up...

much too fast.

The daily doings of kids—from raucous birthday parties to quiet moments adrift in daydreams—have always provided a wellspring of inspiration for my art. I am constantly energized and inspired by the spirit, the purity, the imagination, the sense of adventure, and the wide-eyed wonder that seem to exist uniquely and universally in children. Kids are silly, sweet, messy, mischievous, trusting, playful, and—without even knowing it—often remind us weary grown-ups the importance of enjoying life and treating each other gently.

In this little book,
I've tried to capture some
of the endless ways that
children bring warmth
into our hearts and light
into the world. As
every parent knows,
childhood is fleeting, but
children provide enough
happy memories to last
a lifetime. That's just
what kids do.

Mary Engelbreit

what kids do...

make sure
everyone's included.

what kids do...

never give up.

what kids do...

like to wrap
their own gifts.

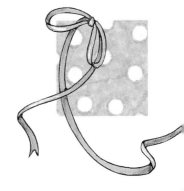

like reading a favorite book
over and over again.

what kids do...

take pride in their work.

seldom clean
their rooms.

what kids do...

have no fear.

what kids do...

really know how to party.

what kids do…

give the best hugs.

what kids do...

take care of their
brothers and sisters.

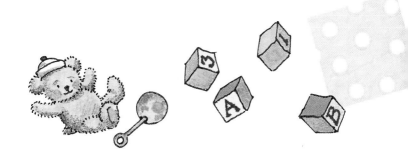

what kids do...

*love watching the same video
over and over...*

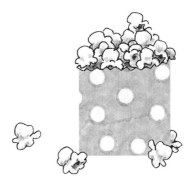

what kids do…

tell it like it is.

what kids do...

know who to seek
for comfort.

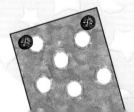

what kids do…

*make the best of
a gray day.*

what kids do...

put their heart
into all they do.

what kids do...

know who their heroes are.

what kids do...

never forget their first loves.

what kids do…

(sometimes) don't mind
going to school.

what kids do...

wait for the tooth fairy.

what kids do...

get themselves into the most
delicious messes.

don't judge books by their covers.

what kids do...

learn from the best teachers.

what kids do...

star in their own shows.

what kids do...

spoil their dinner!

what kids do...

show off.

what kids do...

see the magic in everything.

FOR ME??!!

what kids do...

love playing dress up.

what kids do...

snuggle.